The ABC's of Church

Francine O'Connor
Illustrated by Chris Sharp

LIGUORI
PUBLICATIONS

One Liguori Drive
Liguori, MO 63057-9999
(314) 464-2500

Imprimi Potest:
Richard Thibodeau, C.SS.R.
Provincial, Denver Province
The Redemptorists

Imprimatur:
+ Paul Zipfel, V.G.
Auxiliary Bishop, Archdiocese of St. Louis

ISBN 0-7648-0024-8
Library of Congress Catalog Card Number: 96-75982
Copyright © 1997, Francine O'Connor
Illustrations © 1997, Liguori Publications

Printed in the United States of America
01 00 99 98 97 5 4 3 2 1
First edition

Cover illustration and design by Chris Sharp

is for the Altar,
the table of God,
where God's people gather
to be one family and share
God's love.

B is for the Bells
   of Sunday morn:
tiny bells that ring at
   Communion time,
and great tower bells that
   call us to Mass.

4

is for the Candles winking
      on the altar,
bright holy lights
      that tell us,
"Jesus is the light
      of the world."

 is for the Deacon,
chosen to serve,
who reads us the
Gospel, baptizes
babies,
and helps us in
countless ways.

E is for the Eucharist,
   that special meal
where bread and wine
   become body and blood,
and we receive Jesus
   in our hearts.

7

 is for the Family of God,
who kneel with us and
sing with us
and pray with us at
every Mass.

 is for the Good News of
Jesus' promise
that "whenever you
come together to pray,
I will be there in
your midst."

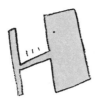 is for the Holy Water
    at the door.
We dip in our fingers and
    sign the cross
in the name of the Father,
    Son, and Holy Spirit.

I is for the Incense burned
on special days.
As the sweet smoke rises
heavenward,
our prayers rise up to
God's throne.

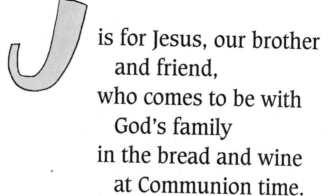

is for Jesus, our brother
   and friend,
who comes to be with
   God's family
in the bread and wine
   at Communion time.

K is for the Kiss (or sign) of Peace.
"Peace be with you," our neighbor says,
and "Peace be with you," we return.

is for the Lectors who read
  the words
that God and Jesus want
  us to hear.
We listen, we learn, and
  we love our Lord.

 is for the Mass, our very
    special time
to worship God, to share
    our faith,
and to receive Jesus in
    our hearts.

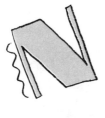 is for God's holy Names,
Father, Son, and Spirit too,
those names we say in
every prayer.

16

is for the Offering
   of the people.
We give to God just
   a little part
of the blessings God has
   given to us.

P is for the Priest who
prepares our Eucharist
and speaks the words
that Jesus spoke:
"This is my body; this is
my blood."

 is for our Quiet Time,
to visit with Jesus
    after Communion,
to thank him for coming
    into our hearts.

R is for our Responses
   to the priest.
When he says,
   "The Lord be with you,"
we respond, "And
   also with you."

S is for the special Songs
    we sing:
songs of happiness,
    songs of love,
songs of praise for Jesus,
    our King.

21

is for the Tabernacle,
   where we keep
   the blessed bread
   that is Jesus,
   and where the light of
   his love ever shines.

 is for the Ushers, who
    are always there
to greet us with smiles
    and show us our seats,
and pass the basket for
    our gifts to God.

is for the robes we
call Vestments,
worn by the priests and
deacons at Mass
to remind us that this
is a holy event.

W is for the
stained-glass
Windows
where pictures of holy
women and men
sparkle and shine with
God's own light.

is for the CROSS of Jesus,
who suffered and died and
rose again
to forgive us and give us
everlasting life.

 is for YOU, the finest word
   in this book.
YOU are God's treasure,
   YOU give God joy,
YOU are the reason God
   gathers the Church.

is for the Zillion
other things
that you will learn
about our Church
while growing up
as a child of God.

About the Author

Francine O'Connor has been entertaining little ones with her lively verse stories of the Bible and the Christian faith for over twenty years. A prolific author, O'Connor has written numerous "ABC" books, including the best-selling *The ABC's of the Mass, The ABC's of the Rosary, The ABC's of the Sacraments, The ABC's of the Ten Commandments,* and *The ABC's of Prayer.* Her "ABC's of Faith" column continues to be one of the most popular features in the *Liguorian* magazine. Until her retirement, she was the coordinator of the children's church at Sts. Peter and Paul parish in St. Louis and also gave lectures and workshops in writing for children. The mother of three and the grandmother of ten, O'Connor has a personal "test-market" for her work. She lives on the family farm in Norfolk, New York, where she continues to write and publish for children.

Other books by Francine O'Connor...

THE ABC'S OF CHRISTMAS

In lively rhyme and verse style, this book leads 3- to 8-year-olds through the traditional stories of Christmas. Each illustrated story entertains and excites children as they learn the true meaning of Christmas. **Hardcover. $14.95**

THE ABC'S OF THE TEN COMMANDMENTS...FOR CHILDREN

This fun little book tailors the Ten Commandments to children and shows them how the commandments apply to their own lives. **$3.95**

THE ABC'S OF THE ROSARY... FOR CHILDREN

By bringing the story of Mary and Jesus to life through verse and illustrations, this book highlights each of the 15 mysteries to help children understand and pray the rosary. **$3.95**

YOU AND GOD

Friends Forever

Using artwork, creative analogies, and simple text, this booklet helps children develop a Catholic identity and a lasting faith. **$3.95**

Order from your local bookstore or write to
Liguori Publications
Box 060, Liguori, MO 63057-9999
(Please add $2 postage and handling to prepaid orders under $9.99; $3 to orders between $10 and $14.99; and $4 to orders $15 and over.)